I0487622

"I read this book cover to cover in one sitting – it was that good! It's funny and fast moving which is unusual for a 'money book.' David's taken away the excuse of 'money and finance is too complicated' from people's stepping up to being rich. To me, there's only two classes of people who shouldn't buy and read (and I should say devour) this book…billionaires and folks who really enjoy suffering and scraping by."
-Steve Swanson, The Barron of Bargains
www.SaveThousandsOnDiamonds.com

"I was a landlord for over 18 years, and I got tired of dealing with irresponsible tenants. Following David's blueprint I was able to retire in only 3 and a half months, and now I don't have to work or deal with those tenants any more. Thanks David!"
-Vilma Vitiello, retired landlord, Clearwater FL

"What has impressed me about David Newby is his commitment to stand behind his word and also to provide ideas for investment which can give great returns. One just such investment gave me a 50% return in 4 months."
-Minesh Baxi, business coach and author of "Top 10 Blunders Business Owners Make"
www.MBaxi.com

"When I first met Dave 10 years ago, I knew he had the thinking and characteristics of a Winner. He not only resolved my cpu issues, but he also offered several ideas to keep everything operating efficiently. When you read this book, you will learn ways to keep your finances operating more efficiently. Dave is one of those people that 'Makes things Happen;' reading this book just may make BETTER things happen in your finances."
-J.P. Masouras, business owner and Futures Trader

Why Didn't Anyone *Teach* Me This Crap?!?!

*There's a 95.7% chance you were raised to be poor;
here's the financial education you never got to join
the 5% of society that's RICH*

by

David Newby

Published by Rock Solid Financial Group LLC
Southfield, MI

Why Didn't Anyone Teach Me This Crap?

©2006 by Rock Solid Financial Group LLC
All rights reserved.

Reproduction or translation of any part of this work beyond that
permitted by Section 107 or 108 of the 1976 United States Copyright Act
without permission of the copyright owner is unlawful. Requests for
permission or further information should be addressed to Rock Solid
Financial Group LLC.

This publication is designed to provide accurate and authoritative
information in regard to the subject matter covered.

It is sold with the understanding that the publisher is not engaged in
rendering legal, accounting or other professional services. If legal advice
or other expert assistance is required, the services of a competent
professional person should be sought.
-From a Declaration of Principles jointly adopted by a Committee of the
American Bar Association and a Committee of Publishers and Associates.

ISBN: 978-1-4303-0977-2

Paperback Edition
131 pages

Rock Solid Financial Group LLC offices located at:

3319 Greenfield Rd. #369, Dearborn MI 48120

I dedicate this book to my wife, Rhea, and my sons Benjamin and Simon. Your presence in my life has helped me rise above my fears and commit 100% to live a life of passion.

And to my Mom Violet who taught me to enjoy this adventure we call life.

Maraming salamat!
(Thank You *in Filipino*)

Table Of Contents

Foreword

David Newby has a dream. Like everybody, his dream was to make a better life for himself and his family. David knew that there were as many ways to make that happen as people trying. Long work days, entrepreneur ventures, corporate ladders, buying lotto tickets were ways to pursue your dreams. All approaches David knew were very different...but the dream remains the same. All dreamers seek something better.

David knew that working for someone else would make reaching his goals and dreams difficult. Normally, you can scrape by while building someone else's business, but to really make it big, David took the leap of faith to do it on his own. Years ago, this spunky kid from Detroit, Michigan, began reaching out to others who could help him reach his dreams.

He knew at a young age that setting goals was not enough. He had to write his goals, review them morning and night, and seek assistance from people and groups who could help him climb to a greater level of success.

I was fortunate and am proud to be one of his mentors. I recall my first contact with him when David's relentless pursuit of me convinced me to admit him into my elite one on one life-long mentoring program. I observed from the start the qualities of a determined winner. It is rare for such a young man to possess these qualities but I was not to judge him, but to move David to a higher level of success. Through real estate investing, his leap of faith had begun backed by his personal faith and that of his family.

David Newby's achievements and accomplishments are chronicled in this, his first book which I am honored to write his foreword to and "introduce him to the world."

Since I first met David, he has continued to grow and expand his business success which has impacted his financial growth. But most important, he has helped countless numbers of people reach their personal/ financial goals. You see, David's ladder of success is built on strong principles of helping others to achieve their goals. David's knowledge transcends his age and his net worth reflects his achievements, not just on paper but in real life.

Realizing his dreams of making a better life for himself and his family, it's easy for me to see his amazing success. David's goal has also been to help others locally, nationally, and worldwide.

This book is for you if you are ready to make the big leap of faith towards your own success. If you're now ready to fulfill your dreams, you have picked up the right book to set you on course. Congratulations to you and I encourage you to read on......your financial destiny is in your hands.

-John Ulmer
National Authority on Buying &
Selling Single Family Homes.
Consultant, Speaker, & Author
Backed by over 5000 Real Estate Deals
www.JohnUlmer.com

Introduction

Hi! My name is David Newby. As a child I was so hyper doctors told my mom to put me on Ritalin; I stuttered a lot and peed the bed until age 10. We lived on welfare in my formative years and my mom, brother, and I survived on $503 a month.

We moved 46 times by the time I turned 17 (mostly to hide from my brother's dad who tried to kill our mom), and my mom had three husbands while I grew up. The only constant in my life for many years was change. I was a bully as a kid and have sat in the back of a police car more than once. I got laid off from my first full time job after 3.5 years and lost my second job after 2 years.

Not exactly the picture of success, is it?

No, it's not. But I overcame all those obstacles and succeeded in spite of them. I utilized the fact that I got laid off at such a young age to decide to make myself layoff-proof for life. And you can utilize whatever obstacles you're facing right now to drive you towards your own success.

You've been programmed for failure with money and finances your whole life, and you probably didn't know it. It's not your parents' or your teachers' or your relatives' fault- they taught you the best they could. But if you look at the average person's finances, they're not that good. I figure you bought this book because you want to do better than average, and I commit to help you with that.

In this book, I'm going to share with you some startling facts about money and how you can get more of it. I'm also going to show you ways to make it grow rapidly and safely, and I'll show you ways to make your money work hard for you so you don't have to keep working hard for money!

Most importantly, I'm going to show you ways to protect the money you already have and all the money you'll ever amass in the future. Sound good to you? What's the point of amassing a fortune only to have it stolen by some jerk that sues you, right?

I can almost guarantee that if you take action and implement what you learn in this book, you will become wealthy. How can I make such a guarantee? Simple- if you do what the rich do, you'll have what the rich have. Do what you've always done, and you'll get the same results you've always got.

If you're going to live, why not live richly in every area of your life? I have no interest in "just scraping by" and neither should you! Being rich begins with a choice. Are you willing to commit to your own success now?

If you are, then you're reading the right book. I don't claim to have all the answers, but I do have a blueprint for success that anyone can follow. Again, you WILL become wealthy using the strategies in this book- that is, if you don't let your fears get the best of you.

After reading this book you will have the basic tools necessary to become rich. I'll expose secrets the rich use to get wealthy.

You'll learn…

- The five most dangerous trends facing your finances today

- Why following conventional wisdom is making you poor

- The good, bad, and the ugly truth about consumer debt;

- How to make yourself layoff-proof for life;

- How to live the life you always wanted but didn't think you could afford;

- The simple steps to build wealth faster than a speeding bullet;

- How to protect your wealth now and for your family's future generations.

Before we get to the good stuff on getting rich, it's important that you understand how messed up our finances are in America. Once you know how severe the problem is, I trust you'll be motivated to do something about it in your own life like I was.

Once you know there's a problem, then you can create a solution and implement it. I'm sure you're ready to implement your own solution to become wealthy, so let's get started and get right to the heart of the problem we're facing in America.

Chapter 1- Something's Wrong With the U.S.A....

In 1992, Aerosmith released a song called "Living on the Edge" with the opening line "Something's wrong with the world today..."

When it comes to Americans' finances, there's DEFINITELY something wrong. Don't take my word for it- see what Uncle Sam has to say:

(According to the U.S. Department of Labor- http://www.bls.gov/)
- Around the age of 60-65 when people retire, their income drops to ½ to 1/3 of what they were barely surviving on when they were working.

* What will your quality of life be if you have to live on that little money when you retire? *

- At age 65, out of every 100 Americans:
  - 1   is Rich
  - 8   are Well-to-do
  - 14   are <u>still</u> Working
  - 24   are Dead
  - 53   are Dead… BROKE!

*that means out of every 100 Americans, only 9 retire in comfort. 91% of all Americans retire dead broke or are still working!

- The average American has over $6,000 of consumer debt and the total debt load has risen from 80% to 93% of disposable income in the past decade.

- Americans on average have a -2% to -5% savings rate. How long can people keep on spending more than they make? If you are in this situation, how long will it be before you're filing bankruptcy?

- Of the 1.5 to 2 million people filing bankruptcy annually, 86% of their marriages end in divorce.

- The total wealth of the average American at age 50 is <u>under</u> $40,000.

9 out of 10 Americans retiring broke, less and less savings for people, more bankruptcies

leading to divorce and broken homes, and more and more debt piling up on us.

It doesn't add up to a pretty picture, does it?

I wish that was all, but there's actually more bad news you should be aware of...

- Since 1974, it has been legal for companies to bankrupt pension plans with no recourse from the employees. Steel companies did it in the 1980s, and in the early 2000s airlines and auto companies are cutting or wiping out retirement benefits. What will you do to protect your pension from this fate?

- 401Ks have replaced pension plans, and the average 401K balance is under $25,000. Most people are not saving enough in their 401Ks to retire comfortably.

- To add the icing on the cake, our government is over $60 Trillion in debt. Divide that out and that equals $240,000 in debt for every man, woman, and child in America. Up until 1985, we were a net lending nation- we loaned out more than we borrowed from other countries. We've amassed all this debt in the last 20 years.

It's 2006, and I live in metro Detroit. I've lived here almost 12 years, and I'm witnessing the disappearance of the middle class American Dream right before my eyes. In the last 3 months alone, Ford, GM, and Delphi have announced over 50,000 layoffs.

GM workers are seeing the writing on the wall and over 22,000 of them have accepted GM's "early buyout" offer of $70,000 to $140,000 in lieu of working for a job or retirement benefits that may or may not be there in a couple years. I think they made a smart move.

I invest in real estate, and Detroit already has lots of foreclosures; with all the layoffs coming, the number of foreclosures in metro Detroit will likely skyrocket the next couple years. It's pretty hard to pay bills with <u>no</u> income and <u>no</u> savings. It's going to get ugly.

I recently met with a homeseller Sarah (*all names in my stories have been changed to protect the identities of those involved. All other information is factual) who works for Ford.

Many in her plant have already been laid off, and she's barely paying her bills now as her overtime has been cut and she's a single mother.

If she gets laid off she'll be bankrupt in 1 month. She recently had a heart attack from the financial stress she's under.

I wish Sarah's situation was the exception to the rule, but sadly it's not. According to government statistics, most Americans are only 30 to 60 days away from bankruptcy if their income was to stop.

If you had to pay 100% of your bills with 53% of your income (unemployment pay), how long would you last?

These statistics may have you a bit concerned, really worried, or you may be saying "Dave, this stuff really isn't that important to me." No matter how you feel about the facts, I have a few questions for you.

1. When will you be financially free? (have you accepted the idea that you'll always be in debt to someone?)

2. If you lost your job, how long could you survive before you ran out of cash?

3. When will you have more time for your family? For yourself?

4. How much more stress can you take?

Financial stress is the #1 cause of divorce, and with a -2% savings rate more and more

Americans are getting stressed financially. Not since the Depression in the 1930s have we had a savings rate this low.

How did we get to this point? We're in the richest, greatest nation on the Earth and 9 out of 10 people retire broke. Despite all the money people are making we're experiencing record bankruptcies, and most people are only 30-60 days away from bankruptcy.

It doesn't all seem to add up, does it? Actually, it does when you understand our education system and the blueprint for failure we've been given.

Let's see where we've been led wrong…

Chapter 2- Why Conventional Wisdom Sucks

Let's see here. To recap from Chapter 1, most people are broke and 9 out of 10 will retire broke or still be working at age 65.

I'm sure you agree with me that most people don't want to end up with that financial future. For <u>you</u> to avoid being one of the 9 who retire broke, it's important to look into what most people do during their life to end up with those horrible results. Then I'll show you how to avoid that fate for yourself.

Would you agree MOST people follow conventional wisdom? Most do.

What is the conventional wisdom about work and money? Go to school and get a good education. Get a safe, secure job and work hard at your career. Invest your 401Ks and IRAs in mutual funds. Retire in comfort and enjoy your golden years. That's what we're taught, right?

How about our education system? Are we taught any vital financial skills we'll need as adults?

Are we taught how to balance a checkbook, make a budget, the importance of savings, how to understand and manage our credit, or how to invest wisely?

We're taught NONE of these important skills, and sadly most parents aren't teaching these skills to their kids because they weren't taught them. It's a failed system, and it needs to change.

Recently, I was at an investor conference and met a couple principals from Utah. The state of Utah has enacted as of fall 2006 a new class on financial literacy that teaches basic financial skills to high school juniors. This is phenomenal and I think every state in America needs to follow Utah's wonderful example. If you're past high school age and you're reading this, consider this book your Financial Matters 101 course you never got!

I contend that a lot of work needs to be done in our lives, because even in the 1950's when Americans saved 10-20% of their income over 90% of people still retired broke. If following that formula leaves 9 out of 10 people broke at age 65, don't you think the plan should be scrapped?!? I sure do.

If conventional wisdom leads people to such crappy results, why do most people keep following it? Simple: most of us haven't been taught how to act any better financially.

We can look around and see that most people are broke, and we don't want that. We can see that most people have a lot of debt and are very stressed financially, and we don't want that. It's no wonder most people are broke- we hardly ever meet people who aren't!!!

We're simply modeling the behavior around us, as poor as it is. What else are we to do?

First of all, admit to yourself that maybe there's a better way of thinking about things. Before you can ever get rich, you need to start with an open mind and admit to yourself that what you already know isn't the "whole truth" – accept that there is more you need to learn.

Rich people aren't any smarter than you or I. They simply are living their lives based on different information than 90% of the population.

The good news for you is that rich people don't have a monopoly on the right information! It's available to you and me; all we have to do is show a little initiative and commit to learning what the rich know.

I asked you earlier if you are committed to living richly. If you are, then say these words with me: "I commit to being rich in every way- my finances, my health, and my spirituality. I commit to learning <u>whatever</u> I need to learn and implementing it until I achieve my desired goal."

Did you just repeat those words out loud with me? If you did, then you just basically agreed with me that conventional wisdom sucks! It's <u>very</u> unconventional to decide to be wealthy- 9 out of 10 people never do.

I want to point out here that you don't have to want to be "wealthy" to repeat the above statement. You can define rich simply as **not** having to work or being broke at age 65; do that and you're richer than 90% of people!

Most people will never make the simple decision to be wealthy. Maybe they were taught that money is bad or that money is the root of all evil (the Bible verse says the LOVE of money is the root of all evil, *not* money itself) or that they don't deserve it.

All of those things are false and limiting beliefs. Maybe you heard such things from your parents or others while you were growing up. Ask yourself: what were the financial results of the people who said those things? Do you want those results? If you don't, chose to respectfully disagree with those limiting beliefs.

I said in the introduction that you were lied to your whole life about money. You weren't lied to maliciously to harm you; you simply weren't given the whole story. You were told "the truth" according to the mediocre masses.

If you want better results financially it makes sense to learn some new truths. What you believe is true for you, and no one can change that.

If I give you a step-by-step formula to become a millionaire in the next 7 years and you tell yourself you can't do it, guess what? You're right! You can't! But if you tell yourself you can do it and you will, you're STILL right! So why not go ahead and choose to believe that your dreams are possible for you since you choose your beliefs anyways?

So, are we in agreement that conventional wisdom sucks? Following it 90% guarantees you'll be retiring in mediocrity leaving many of your life's dreams unfulfilled.

Are we also in agreement that there are different sets of "truths" out there and that you can <u>choose</u> your truths? Good. Isn't it cool to know if you grew up poor or middle class you can choose to adopt the mindset of the rich in order to become rich? Awesome!

So, once you've accepted the fact that most of us were taught a formula for financial failure, what do you do about it? Go buy a course off late-night TV? Go to a real estate or stock trading seminar?

Before you do any of that, I want to make sure I help you condition your mind for optimal results when you do start taking some new actions. A key element to reconditioning your mind is to understand your money blueprint.

Your Money Blueprint: Your money blueprint is the way you were taught to think about and act with money. The majority of our money blueprint we learned from our parents' examples. Sadly, we often have incorrect thinking about money we learned from our parents.

To give you an example, the last couple years I've started to make what I consider to be "good money" but I noticed a disturbing trend. I could make 4 or 5 times what my family needed to pay our bills for the month, but the money didn't last 4 or 5 months. After only 2 months, we'd be getting tight on money again!

I couldn't figure out why this kept happening until I learned the concept of the money blueprint. Growing up on welfare, we were always "just getting by" every month on $503. There was always just enough to pay the bills and little extra. If we had a little extra money at the end of the month, we would go to the arcade or go to the $1 movie.

I was programmed to "just get by" and that's what I was doing as an adult. If I made $20,000 extra in a month, I'd find a way to spend that money so I could "just get by" the next month. I was doing whatever was necessary so my lifestyle matched how I saw myself subconsciously. Thank God I learned what I was doing to myself and my family!

I was sabotaging myself and my family in order for my life to coincide with how I saw myself on the inside. I've been doing it my whole adult life, and now that I'm aware of that money blueprint flaw I'm correcting it.

My wife's father died suddenly when she was 10 years old, and her family's lifestyle went from living comfortably to just getting by. My mother-in-law invested in several businesses but struggled financially for many years.

As a result, my wife invests extra money in things that will have value in the future but produce little income- things like land that we can build on or sell later. She's looking to fill the security void that was created when her father died while at the same time not producing too much income like her mom's investments did.

What is your money blueprint? How were you taught to interact and think towards money growing up? It's essential you figure out your money blueprint and make sure you're not sabotaging yourself in order to improve your life financially.

A great resource to help you find out your own money blueprint is a book *"Secrets of the Millionaire Mind"* by T. Harv Eker.

(www.MillionaireMindBook.com) I can't recommend you read it highly enough.

What formula for handling money and working should we replace the one we were taught with? Good question.

It took me over 5 years of searching high and low to discover my blueprint for success, and it all started with me changing my thinking. Changing your thinking doesn't just happen overnight.

Let's look at the truths of the rich and how we can adopt them for our benefit. Let's look deeper into how the rich think so we can join them on the beach in the Bahamas… on our yachts in Monaco… in first class on the way to our favorite vacation spot…

PRACTICAL EXERCISES FOR THIS CHAPTER:

(Fill in <u>your</u> dreams here! Don't be afraid to dream and be let down- if you shoot for the moon you just may end up among the stars.)

Write Out Your Dream Lifestyle (where you'll live, the car you'll drive, what you'll do with your time- be as **specific** as possible):

_____

_____

_____

_____

_____

_____

_____

_____

_____

_____

_____

_____

Read this every night before you go to bed and visualize living this lifestyle in as much detail as possible. This technique is called Psycho-Cybernetics and has been used by over 30 million people to change their life.

Exercise: Improve YOUR Money Blueprint
First, write your CURRENT beliefs about
money. Be honest about limiting beliefs.

_____

_____

_____

_____

_____

_____

Write how you will CHANGE how you think
about and handle money- your **new blueprint**

_____

_____

_____

_____

_____

_____

_____

_____

**Read your new blueprint daily as you wake
up in the morning. Changing your beliefs
is a key step on your journey to becoming
rich. Try these 2 exercises for just 30 days
and see what a difference they make!**

Chapter 3- Let YOUR Blueprint For Success Begin… NOW!

By now you know we're in bad shape financially as Americans. You also know that we've been lied to, undereducated about how to handle money, and given a blueprint for financial failure.

You're ready to hear me expose the secrets to getting rich, and you may be asking yourself: "What are you talking about- think like the rich? Just tell me the first secret already!" Alrighty then!

Here's Secret #1:
The rich think differently about money and work than the poor and middle class.

The first action you need to take on your road to wealth is to change the way you think about work and money. Why? Consider this simple formula.

Beliefs → Thoughts → Actions → Results.

Our beliefs lead to our thoughts. Our thoughts lead to our actions. And our actions produce our results.

How can we start to think like the rich? By rejecting beliefs we were taught growing up that are limiting and keep us from becoming wealthy.

It's critical you adopt the thoughts and beliefs of the rich in order to get their results. If you don't, you'll NEVER be wealthy.

Here's an example. Poor people and middle class people often say, "I can't afford it." Rich people ask, "*How* can I afford it?"

A talk I had with a friend illustrates this point well. I've know Bob several years. Bob is a smart guy and already owned two rental properties by the time he was 25. They were both paying him a nice extra income until he had a problem with one of his tenants.

He ended up losing one of the properties to foreclosure and had a blemish on his credit. Bob was telling me he wanted to buy more investment properties as soon as his credit improved.

I too had some blemishes on my credit, and while Bob was waiting for his credit to improve I bought 5 properties. I told Bob a couple ways he could buy properties even

with his damaged credit, but he hasn't yet.
He's still waiting for his credit to improve.

What was the difference between me and
Bob? We both had damaged credit and we
both wanted to buy investment real estate.

The only difference was our thinking. Bob
chose to think like the masses ("I can't afford
it") and I chose to think like the rich and
found a way to buy several properties despite
my bad credit.

Two books I highly recommend that helped
me learn to think like the wealthy are *"Think
and Grow Rich"* by Dr. Napoleon Hill and
"Rich Dad Poor Dad" by Robert Kiyosaki.

You can download a FREE copy of *"Think
and Grow Rich"* at the following website:
www.FinancialSuccessBlueprint.com/CrapBook.html

There are several important truths you need to learn in order to become rich. Most of them are found in the two books I just mentioned, but I want to highlight a few key truths for you to think over. See how many of the limiting beliefs of the poor and middle class you've had in the past that you are now replacing with the truths of the rich.

The Poor and middle class think:	The Rich think:
"I have to work hard to make a lot of money."	"It's easy to create as much wealth as I want."
"Inheriting money or winning the lotto are the two most likely ways to get rich."	"Building businesses and investing the profits is the best way to create wealth."
"The rich are greedy."	"I'm just like everyone else."
"I'd rather have love than money."	"It's not an either/or world- it's an AND world."
"It's hard to get rich."	"It's easy to create wealth."
"If someone's getting rich, someone else is losing money and getting poor."	"There is infinite wealth that can be created- there's more than enough for everyone."

Did you find you believe some of the thoughts
of the poor and middle class? If you did,
that's OK. Several years ago I thought many
of those beliefs, and I'm glad to tell you I've
learned to think like the rich- and so can you!

I encourage you to think seriously about your
belief system and how it relates to money.
Realize that money in and of itself is neither
good or bad- it's simply a tool. You can use it
for good to help yourself and those around
you or you can use it for bad. Someone may
have bad intentions of what they want to do
with money, but that doesn't make money
itself bad. The problem is with their heart.

So if you know your heart is in the right
place, don't feel bad about wanting a lot of
money. Also it's important to realize that

money itself will neither make you happy or sad.

Many people think they will be happier when they have a lot of money. That usually isn't the case! Learn to be content where you are right now, and still pursue your dreams. If you can't be content right now you'll never be content no matter how much money you have.

The rich realize that money is a tool and they usually aren't that emotionally attached to it. The less you "need" it, the more of it you often end up having.

So be empowered! You now know that money is neither good nor bad and it's OK to want a lot of it. You can be content now knowing you're on the path to pursuing your dreams and as you create more wealth for yourself you'll fulfill those dreams.

Rich people also realize that money does not define who they are. They are who they are and wealth is attracted to them. Wealth comes to those who attract it, and being confident in who you are and feeling deserving of wealth are two key beliefs you need to have to become rich.

I know a gentleman who does consulting for some of the most powerful people in America- Oprah, Larry Ellison of Oracle, and Bill Gates to name a few. Do you think if they lost all their money tomorrow they'd stay broke? NO WAY! They know they bring great value to the world, they're confident in who they are, and they'd have their wealth back in no time.

Well, guess what? You're just as valuable as they are. KNOW that you bring great value to the world, be confident in who you are, and wealth will be more attracted to you!

If you look for fulfillment or validation from money, you'll find that it will often come up short in doing that for you. Many multi-millionaires and billionaires have committed suicide; the billionaire Howard Hughes died a paranoid, lonely man.

There are many examples all throughout history of this- just know that money isn't a cure-all and that most wealthy people have problems just like you!

Remember- money is simply a tool, you don't have to be emotionally attached to it or wrap your self-worth up in how much of it you have, and you deserve to be wealthy and to have the life that wealth can afford you.

I encourage you to write down the limiting beliefs you have about money on a chart and then to the right write down your new beliefs you're replacing the old limiting beliefs with. Say aloud, "I used to believe (limiting belief), but now I know (new empowering belief)."

To get maximum value from this exercise, put this chart where you will see it daily. This may seem silly or unimportant to you, but remember a couple things: rich people do what others are unwilling to do. They also are usually growing as people and seek to learn from those who have success. So be willing to grow and do this exercise even if it seems silly to you at first.

Napoleon Hill talked of this principal in his book *"Think and Grow Rich"* and T. Harv Eker's book *"Secrets of the Millionaire Mind"* has several online tools you can use to develop a millionaire mindset. Again, you can download *"Think and Grow Rich"* at www.FinancialSuccessBlueprint.com/CrapBook.html for FREE and I recommend you buy Harv Eker's book **just** for the great tools he gives you online to hone your mind to attract wealth.

To recap from this chapter, Wealth Secret #1 is you MUST begin to think about work and money differently if you want to be the most successful person you can be. We focused a lot on money thinking; what about work?

WHY DIDN'T ANYONE *TEACH* ME THIS CRAP?

Chapter 4- Job Security? Yeah, right!

In the last chapter, we covered how Wealth Secret #1 is that the rich think differently about money and work than the poor and middle class. We focused on belief systems about money mainly, and now it's time to look into how the rich think about work.

Let's look at what most people are taught about work first. "Get a good education, get a safe secure job, save for the future, and you can retire comfortably." The second part of that equation is "get a safe secure job."

That's conventional wisdom, and remember that conventional wisdom leaves 91% of people broke or still working at age 65. That <u>sucks</u> if you ask me.

Let me tell you how I discovered this whole mantra of "get a safe secure job" was exposed as a lie to me. When I finished college as an x-ray technician, I moved to metro Detroit Michigan to get to know my dad better.

I got my first full time x-ray job about 3 months later. It was a cool job doing portable x-rays in nursing homes, and I met my wife (a nurse) at one of the nursing homes through my job. (Hooray for Filipinas!)

The company I worked for was losing a lot of market share to their competitor due to poor management of their relationships with their clients, and I got laid off. I was in the top 20% of my 26 coworkers in overall performance but I was let go suddenly without warning. "We have to let you go, Dave." Bam! No warning. Job gone.

Imagine my shock- I was among the top 5 workers for performance! I had worked there 3.5 years! I wasn't the low man on the totem pole; there were several people who had been hired after me! It wasn't a unionized company where I get let go because I had little seniority. Wasn't this America where you get judged on your performance?!

You may or may not have experienced the "thrill" of being laid off, but I'm sure you know someone who has. The bottom line is that I learned very early on that the idea of job security is just that- an idea. And an idea whose time has past, by the way. At the time I got laid off I was mad about it. But now I see it as one of the best things that ever happened to me.

Being laid off made me mad enough to decide I was going to learn how to be "layoff-proof." I didn't know how at the time, but I made the decision to learn how to not need a job.

The fact of the matter is that job security is a thing of the past. The days where you worked for a company for 30-45 years and then retired with a pension are over. The average worker today has 3-4 different CAREERS over their 40 year work history, and pensions are dying out quickly. Furthermore, companies are <u>bankrupting</u> existing pension funds at an alarming rate!

Job security was an idea that came to be popular during the industrial age. Before the industrial age most people were small business owners, and that was only 5 generations ago.

Now the industrial age is coming to a close. Throughout the 1900s the #1 company in the world was always a manufacturer. Now in 2006 the #1 company in the world is Wal-Mart, and they manufacture nothing. They are a distribution company, and all they make is money!

We're in the Information Age now, and those who can process the vast sea of information flowing around the world quickly to their benefit are the ones getting rich.

So how do the rich think about work? Do they believe in job security? What do they think are the best ways to make a living? The best ways to get rich?

The answers are startling.

The rich don't believe in working hard, first of all. They believe in working smart and having money work hard for them.

Second, they realize you'll never be truly wealthy working for someone else or in your own company where you have to be there for your business to run. **True wealth is having both money <u>and</u> the time to enjoy it.**

An important thing to know is that all people in the world make money one of four ways: as employees, as self-employed, as business owners, or as investors.

Employees work for someone else, and self-employed people have businesses that require them to be there. Examples of self-employed people are Realtors, doctors, and lawyers. If a Realtor doesn't sell a house they don't get

paid. Same for a doctor or lawyer- if they
don't see patients/clients they don't get paid.

Ninety five percent of the people in the world
work as employees or are self-employed.
Guess how much of the money in the world
they control? I've had people tell me 60%,
20%, 80%, 30%. Most people guess too high.
They only control 5% of the world's money!!!
That's crazy, isn't it?

Business owners and investors are only 5% of
the world's population, yet they control 95%
of the world's money.

Why is this?

The answer is simple. Business owners and
investors use the power of leverage to create
wealth while employees and self-employed
people trade hours for dollars.

Business owners leverage business systems to create money. These systems work 80% of the time and will run without them being there. An example of this is a McDonald's franchise. The reason people pay $1 million to own a McDonald's and there's a waiting list to own them is that they have a proven system of running a restaurant profitably.

A true business is one you can leave for a year and it will do as well as or better than it did while you were present. When you use this criteria to analyze most businesses, they don't hold up as true businesses.

Most business owners people think of as successful are self-employed and their businesses that would fall apart if they were gone. Remember- they're fighting over the 5% of the money with 95% of the population! They're not as successful as we were raised to believe. And to think that it was my dream to become a doctor when I was a kid.

Investors leverage money to create more money. Savvy investors know business very well and routinely earn 20% to 40% or much higher consistently on their money. Most investors' money they invest are profits from businesses they own.

Which of the four ways are you making money now? Which way would you prefer to make your living? I haven't had a client yet tell me they don't want to own a true business or be an investor.

In order to go to the right side of the cashflow quadrant you must change your beliefs about work. As you change your beliefs, your thoughts and your actions will follow.

So how do you become a business owner or savvy investor? Commit to learning what the rich know and start thinking like they do. Add action and you have a winning recipe for success. It's imperative that you take action even if you don't feel you're ready. You learn the most from your mistakes, and mistakes are essential to success. Yes, you read that right. Mistakes are <u>essential</u> to success!

Let me give you an example to illustrate my point. I bought my first real estate course when I was 25. I wanted to do real estate deals, but I was afraid to make a mistake on the paperwork and lose what I owned in a lawsuit. I let the fear of loss stop me from pursuing my dream for 4 years.

Then two things happened to me. I got a real estate course by Ron Legrand that explained how to fill out every line of different kinds of real estate contracts, and I went broke. So I knew how to fill out the paperwork and I had no more money to lose! Within 4 months of those two things happening I had quit my job and was a full time real estate investor.

Along the way I made several mistakes on deals and even lost money on some, but those mistakes led me to discover even better business and investment opportunities. Now I'm basically retired because I've automated my businesses and investments and I've learned how to use the power of leverage to work for me in <u>true</u> businesses.

The point is this: if I didn't take action and I didn't make the mistakes I made, I wouldn't be retired at age 32.

So go ahead and start taking some action. Admit your fear to yourself, and take action anyway. Do the thing you fear and the death of fear is certain! The sooner you make your mistakes and learn from them, the sooner you'll get the financial results you want.

A couple key things to remember

If you want to be truly wealthy you want to own true businesses and be a savvy investor. As you're getting ready to take action, do a couple things.

First, seek out mentors in the area of business. You can look for someone local to emulate who is successful in the area of business you want to pursue, and S.C.O.R.E. is a great organization composed of retired executives who can mentor you as you begin your business endeavors. (http://www.Score.org)

Second, always analyze any business opportunity very closely. Ask yourself, "Can this business be automated? Is it automated already? What needs to be done and how quickly can I do it to get this business to run without me being here?"

I know of a very successful businessman who's started and sold over 7 companies who will not start any business unless he can make a plan to automate it and sell it within 3 years. Now that's some good business thinking!

To recap from this chapter, we've learned:

The rich don't work hard for money; they make money work hard for them.

The rich think about money and work very differently than most people. They use the power of leverage in businesses and investments to create more wealth. To become truly wealthy you must become a business owner and investor. To get the whole scoop on thinking like the rich when it comes to making money, I highly recommend you read the book **"The CASHFLOW Quadrant™"** by Robert Kiyosaki. You can buy it at any major bookstore or at http://RichDad.com.

So, do you think making more money as a business owner and investor is the whole solution? Do you remember your "Money Blueprint" from Chapter 1? Let's analyze another key component necessary for financial success.

Chapter 5- "If I only made a little more money…"

We just discussed how the rich think differently about money and work. That's Wealth Secret #1.

Wealth Secret #2: The rich have good self control and don't spend everything they make.

I know it sounds overly simple but a key ingredient to creating wealth and avoiding financial ruin is to have self-control and not spend everything you make. Americans seem to have a hard time following this basic formula for success.

We're spending $1.05 for every $1 we're making, and basic math dictates we can't continue living this way. We're going broke as a nation. Americans as a whole aren't stupid, so why are we doing this?

Our beliefs about saving and debt are out of whack, and we expect others to take care of us when we get old. Our money blueprints have a major flaw, and we need to fix it pronto if we want true financial security.

When I worked as a loan officer, I heard clients say all the time "If I only made $5000 more, I'd be fine financially." "If I made $20,000 more I'd be able to get out of debt." "If I only made $50,000 more a year I'd be able to retire a millionaire."

Delusions delusions delusions. Wake up!! Butthead from the TV show *Beavis and Butthead* would smack them across the face five times and say "Snap out of it!" Making more money will NEVER solve financial problems. You need to learn to live on less than what you make now, no matter how small your income.

If you make $50,000 a year now and spend $52,000 a year, what would happen if you started making $75,000 a year? You'd spend $78,000 a year. Would you be further ahead or further behind? You'd be another $1000 behind!

I've met people who make over $1 million a year and they spend $1.1 million. The answer isn't making more money; start spending less than you make now and you'll be much further off when you start making more. There is a Bible verse that says "He who is faithful with little will be faithful with much." Start being a faithful steward of what you have now and you will be much better off.

It serves you no good to tell yourself you'd save more money if you had a bigger income. If you currently spend all you make and then some, you'd do the same thing with a bigger income. This is due to Perkin's Law, an economic law which states that **"Expenses always rises to meet income."** If you want to become wealthy, you've got to break the law- Perkin's Law, that is!!

If you don't learn to break Perkin's Law in your personal finances, you're headed for financial ruin. You'll retire broke, you'll outlive your money, and you'll end up eating dogfood out of a can when you're old. Social Security (or "Social Insecurity" as I like to call it) likely won't be around to bail you out either. Is this the future you want?

So what can you do to break Perkin's Law in your own finances? First, admit there's a problem. Then, look at your money blueprint (how you think about and interact with money) and improve it. Last, start changing your financial habits today.

1. Admit there's a problem.

Most people like to tell themselves "I'll be fine" and no one likes to admit that they're making mistakes. It's only human nature to want to be right, but when it comes to money we can all benefit from a little humility.

Although 90% of Americans aren't saving enough for retirement, 65% of Americans think they'll be fine financially when they retire. Why are we deluding ourselves?

The good news is that it's not all your fault.
Part of the reason people keep their heads in
the sand when it comes to looking at their
finances is that they don't know where to turn
for solutions. Plus we're creatures of our
environment.

Everywhere we turn, Madison Avenue is
telling us to "Buy it now; you deserve it" and
"Refinance your home so you can buy that
dream car or take that dream vacation."
We're encouraged to make emotional
purchases every day, and it can be hard to
resist the temptation to go into further debt to
buy something with a low monthly payment.

Lastly, our government is encouraging us to
go into further debt! They give us a tax break
to refinance our home and go further into debt
but they don't give us a tax break if we invest

our money. I think the incentives should be the other way around.

(*there's a way to flip the script on Uncle Sam and use those tax breaks to our benefit-you just have to use the debt to buy assets, not liablilities. More on that in the chapter on investing)

So you have financial ignorance, emotional purchases, and our government's tax code adding up to create a financial mess for us. If you want to break this financial cycle in your own life NOW, you must admit there's a problem first of all. Then you can move to step 2.

2. Look at and improve your money blueprint.

Earlier I encouraged you to analyze your money blueprint. I also encouraged you to write down limiting beliefs you've had about money and the new beliefs you're now replacing them with.

Did you do it?

Well, now it's time to take some action. If you just read something, you learn only 10% of it. If you read it and do it, you'll learn 65% of it. If you teach it to someone else, you'll learn 90% of it. So if you want to get maximum benefit out of this book read it, apply it to your finances, and teach the ideas to someone else.

When it comes to your money blueprint, how do you interact and think about money? How can your money blueprint be improved?

Write these things down. Write down
what limiting beliefs you have about
money and harmful ways you interact with
it. Then decide to replace each limiting
belief or harmful way of handling money
with empowering beliefs and wise ways of
handling money. It's not enough to
eliminate something bad; you have to
replace it with something good.

Then share this information with someone
you trust who is willing to hold you
accountable to your improvement.

3. Start changing your financial habits.

There's two sides to this coin- controlling
spending and increasing savings. The first

thing you can change is to get your spending under control. Most people don't keep a budget and don't know if they're spending more than they're making.

If you're not sure if you're spending more than you make, you can write down everything you buy every day on a piece of paper (get receipts and log them every evening on the paper) for a month. If you do it for a whole two months you'll have a very clear picture of where your money is going.

Once you know what you're spending, you can look for needless expenses to reduce in order to start saving. A good goal to shoot for is to be able to save 10% of everything you make. If you're spending more than you make now, don't let that number scare you.

Just start saving what you can, even if it's only $1 a week. Set that money aside in a jar, envelope, or savings account and don't touch it. Once you've developed this habit you'll find it becomes easier to save more. You just need to start the habit and it will get easier and easier. Pretty soon you'll be saving a lot more than you thought you could!

I recommend saving 3-6 months' worth of your monthly expenses in a Survival Account. Your survival account is an account you keep in savings or a money market account for emergencies. If something happens to you you can pay your bills with this money.

I recommend you build your survival account before paying off debts. Many financial coaches and authors say to pay off debts first or pay off debts and build your survival account at the same time. I say this: you can't pay your bills with a paid off car. Or paid off furniture. You can only pay your bills with cash, so have some of it readily available.

Build your survival account first and then pay down debts. Sure, you're going to pay a little more interest on your debt but which is worse: paying a little more interest on your debts or getting hurt/laid off, not being able to work, and falling behind on most of your debts and ruining your credit?

If you pay off your debts first you're looking out for your bank's interests more than your own financial interests. Protect yourself financially first!

Another thing you can do to control your spending is to pay 5% or 10% of your income to your savings account right away when you get paid even if you're not sure what you're currently spending; then you can force yourself to live on the remaining money. Expenses will get cut out of necessity if you follow this model.

Paying yourself first is a big key to financial success. This is Rule #2 of the Rockefeller Rules, a set of financial principles billionaire John D. Rockefeller taught his children. Rule #1 is tithe the first 10% of your income to your church or a charity you believe in, and Rule #2 is pay yourself the second 10% of your income for savings and investment. Guess what Rule #3 is? Track all your expenses! If it's good enough for a billionaire, it should be good enough for us.

I advise you to pay yourself as much as you can first before paying others. No, I'm not suggesting you pay yourself and skip your mortgage payment- that will hurt your credit rating and a good credit rating can be one of your biggest financial assets! (I'll reveal more on this topic in the chapter on investing)

What I am saying is that you should get in the habit of paying yourself as much as possible before paying other bills. You'll have bills as long as you're alive and there will always be unexpected expenses that come up.

Why not just pay yourself first and consider it one of your most important bills? That way you'll have the habit of paying yourself each and every month, and you can become truly rich once you learn how to invest that money wisely.

Chapter Recap: You must spend less than you make if you ever want to get ahead. Making more money is not the solution. Break Perkins' Law in your finances, start paying yourself first, and start tracking your spending so you can find areas to eliminate or reduce expenses. Lastly, get a trusted friend or family member to hold you accountable to improving your finances in the areas of saving and spending.

The target is to get to a point where you're saving 10% of what you make. But is that enough to ensure you'll be financially OK?

Earlier I shared with you that in 1953 Americans were saving 15-20% of their income, yet 90% of them still retired broke at 65. So NO! Saving more isn't enough.

How and where should you invest your money so you can retire rich? Let's examine that, shall we? Nothing gets me more excited.

WARNING!

YOU'RE ABOUT TO READ A CHAPTER THAT WILL LIKELY CHALLENGE YOUR BELIEFS ABOUT WHAT'S POSSIBLE.

REMEMBER THAT TRADITIONAL THINKING HAS BEEN INGRAINED IN YOUR MIND, AND YOU MAY HAVE A KNEE-JERK REACTION TO SOME OF THE STATEMENTS IN CHAPTER 6.

I HAVE ONLY ONE REQUEST:
WHEN YOU READ SOMETHING AND YOUR INITIAL REACTION IS
" *That's* Not Possible,"
SIMPLY ASK YOURSELF
"*HOW* can that be possible?"

AS YOU NOW READ THIS CHAPTER WITH AN OPEN MIND TO NEW POSSIBILITIES, YOU WILL GET MAXIMUM BENEFIT OF IT.

LET'S GET TO IT!

Chapter 6- Traditional Investment Advice Sucks!

"Invest your money in mutual funds. Dollar cost average and buy more every month. Invest for the long haul. Eight to ten percent is the average return you should expect."

Crap crap crap!! That's crappy advice!

That's what we've been taught to do with our investments, and it's a recipe for crappy financial results. Remember that from Chapter 1, nine out of ten Americans retire broke. And those people are following traditional investment advice.

Wealth Secret #3: The rich take control of their investments and don't follow the crowd.

I advocate you MUST go against the crowd and start taking responsibility for your investments if you ever want to retire rich. You must be willing to learn a few new financial skills in order to invest like the wealthy, and you must be able to think outside the box. The results are well worth it!

If you are content to follow traditional advice and give yourself a 9/10 chance of retiring broke, you can skip the rest of this chapter and go to the next. If you want to increase your odds of financial success, read on.

There are three steps to investing like the ultra-wealthy. Invest in protecting what you already have first, invest in high yielding yet safe investments (yes, they do exist!), and invest in your family's future to leave a legacy for generations to come.

Step 1: Invest in protecting yourself

I have a friend named Charles who started investing in real estate about 7 years ago. He got some courses, applied what he learned from them, and built a $1.2 million net worth in only 14 months.

Then a tenant sued him and he lost everything- not just his business but even his personal house! He had to declare bankruptcy. Sadly, this happens to people all across America every day. You don't have to be a business owner to be at risk- there's a 3 in 5 chance you'll be sued in the next 10 years if you live in the good ol' US of A.

What can you do to protect what you have? Invest in protection against lawsuits. There are companies who specialize in asset protection- they help you structure your finances in such a way that you won't lose everything when you get sued like my friend Charles did.

There are even ways to structure your financial affairs so that if someone sued you and won, you <u>wouldn't</u> have to pay them and they'd still have to pay the taxes on their "winnings" as if you <u>did</u> pay them! Too bad Charles didn't know these techniques.

> **You can learn more details about how to protect what you have now and make your assets safe from lawsuits in my Special Report "Insider Secrets Revealed" at** http://FinancialSuccessBlueprint.com/CrapBook.html

Another important asset to protect is the equity in your house. There are two major threats to the equity in your house: inability to make your house payments through a job loss or illness and natural disaster. Most people leave their equity in their house thinking it's safe and it isn't.

When I was a loan officer, a gentleman called me looking for a loan. He had been laid off from his job 3 months earlier and hadn't found a new job yet. I couldn't give him a loan because he didn't have a job. He only owed $150,000 on a house worth $250,000. He "had" $100,000 in equity in his house but he couldn't get to it! He fell behind on his mortgage payments and 4 months later lost it to foreclosure. He lost $100,000 of equity to the bank and his credit was ruined.

Natural disasters can also wipe out equity you have in your home. Countless times peoples' homes have been destroyed only to have the insurance companies find a way to not pay for the damages. So you can lose your home AND the equity you thought was safe in it.

Think this is a rare occurrence? It happens more than you may realize.

What can you do to protect your home equity from these dangers? Refinance your home to as close to 100% of its value as you can.

Don't spend the money when you pull the equity out; invest it prudently and make sure you have easy access to it. That way if you get injured or laid off you can use the money to pay your bills until you get back on your feet. If your home is destroyed by a natural disaster, now the bank is at risk of not getting paid by the insurance company and not you. Don't you like the idea of the bank taking all the risk instead of you? You should!

Now, where should you invest that money where it will be safe and liquid?

Step 2: Invest in high-yielding yet safe investments.

For equity you pull out of your home, there are two options I use. The most common investment that makes sense for most people is Universal Index Life Insurance. You'll pay 6-8% on the money you borrow on your mortgage and you'll earn 6-8% in your insurance policy.

After tax breaks you'll earn a 1-2% return on your money while having easy access to it. You won't get rich that way but you will be in a much safer position. This technique is described in great detail in the book "*Missed Fortune 101*" by Doug Andrews. Little risk little reward.

The second option I use is a real estate backed investment that has yielded an average 30% return the past 28 years (with 6-8% monthly cashflow). The company has never lost money on a single deal in the entire 28 years. Little risk bigger reward. This investment isn't for most people- it can lose money and carries risk like all investments do.

Most people can't handle that when it comes to equity in their home. I've exercised my risk muscle over the last several years so I can handle it. It's not for the faint of heart. ☺

I also routinely take advantage of investments that yield 20% to 80% or higher returns. Most people think this means they are high risk. For me they're not. I see them posing no more bigger risk than mutual funds. Instead of telling yourself, "That's not possible" ask yourself how it's possible.

Let's compare real fast, shall we? Would you rather make a 10% return secured by a company's reputation where it **doesn't** cashflow and you can lose money? Or would you rather make a 30% return secured by real estate where it **does** cashflow 6-8% a year and you can lose money? I'll go with choice #2.

In the late '90s people were euphoric over making 30-40% returns in the stock market. Then the market crashed and wiped out half of most peoples' nest eggs. What if you could consistently earn a higher than normal return without as much risk? It's possible.

Many of my clients do exactly that; they earn 20-30% per year or more secured by real estate, and you can too if you take some time to get the right inside information. You don't have to give up safety to earn a higher rate of return than normal!

The fact of the matter is that if you get educated and become a sophisticated investor you can earn these kinds of high investment returns and mitigate your risk. This is what the ultra-wealthy do. Remember most of us were conditioned to accept 10% average returns- what results does that give us? Being broke at retirement. Thanks but no thanks!

So how do you pass on all your financial education and wisdom once you've become a sophisticated investor?

Step 3: Invest in your family's future by leaving a legacy for future generations.
 It's important to not only learn how to invest like the wealthy but pass this education on to your kids and others to cause lasting change.

There's a phrase in financial circles that says "Shirtsleeves to shirtsleeves in three generations." What it refers to is that someone will roll up their sleeves and make a fortune in the first generation, and three generations later all the money will be gone because their kids squandered it and the great grandkids will have to roll up their sleeves and work again.

What is the best way to prevent the "shirtsleeves to shirtsleeves" phenomenon from occurring in your family? What is the best way to leave a legacy of wealth for your kids and your grandkids and your great grandkids and beyond?

There are two great things you can do to pass on a great financial legacy to your kids. The first is to live a life of balance while you're building wealth. I have a friend whose parents built a $100 million net worth in the 1990s. They were busy and never around, so my coach saw money as bad. It was the thing that kept her parents away from her. No matter how much money you have now or how much you plan to have, live a balanced life while you're pursuing your dreams.

By the way, their parents did not their assets structured properly and lost everything (the whole $100 million!) when they had a few business setbacks. Structuring your assets properly will not only protect you from lawsuits but will protect you from losing everything if you have a business setback as well. My encouragement to you to protect what you have now is crucial.

> **If you haven't already, download my report "Insider Secrets Revealed" at** http://FinancialSuccessBlueprint.com/CrapBook.html **to learn how to fully protect your assets. You'll also learn more about the kinds of investments I utilize to earn 30-80% safely.**

The formula I use for time management comes from my favorite lifestyle coach Marshall Sylver (http://www.Sylver.com). I divide my time equally between programming, profit, and play. Programming is training your mind for optimal performance- reading books. Profit is making a living, and play is time relaxing and having fun with friends and family.

Notice that you should only spend 1/3 of your time working. Is your life out of balance? Seriously consider restructuring your schedule if it is out of balance- for your sake as well as that of your family.

The second thing you can do is to create a Family Bank. A Family Bank is a collection of not only financial assets but other valuable things that have happened in the family. Its purpose is to benefit the whole family so you can learn from each other.

So how can you make deposits and withdrawals from your Family Bank? First, decide on a time when your family will get together each year. Even if your kids are grown, make a strong effort to get together with them for at least a couple days a year to create your Family Bank.

Each person in the family should share what they have learned in the past year regarding money and other areas of life. These are your **deposits** into the Family Bank and should be written down for the benefit of future members of the family. Family members may also deposit actual money into the Family Bank for other family members to use. This money must be paid back and should only be used to financially advance the family (no lending money out of the Family Bank for Junior to buy a new motorcycle!).

Everyone in the family gets to make immediate **withdrawals** out of the Family Bank of the new information they learn when you have your annual Family Bank meeting. Actual withdrawals of cash should be paid back in a timely manner that is agreed upon by all. A responsible member of the family should be the Treasurer of the Family Bank.

Encouragement, trust, and accountability are all key ingredients necessary to make your Family Bank as wealthy as possible.

You can have your Family Bank meetings
more often than annually if you want. If your
children live with you, you may want to host
Family Bank meetings once every 6 months.
Schedule at least a day of fun relaxing activity
for your family to enjoy when you have your
Family Bank meetings. Add some play to the
mix and your kids will more likely reattend!

Another thing you can do to leave a better
legacy for your family and others is to think
about how you can support the causes that are
dearest to your heart. We can learn a lot from
the example of Bill Gates and Warren Buffet,
the two richest men in the world in 2006.

They aren't leaving all their money to their
kids so they can live high off the hog.
They're leaving nice sums for their heirs and
giving the rest to charity. This is the ultimate
in estate planning- leaving an inheritance for

your kids, grandkids, and the world around you! It's a pretty cool idea to aspire to, isn't it? What charities or causes are dear to your heart? How'd you like to be able to support the charities you care about even after you're dead? You can if you structure things right.

Once your immediate income needs and your retirement income needs are met (including a budget to have lots of fun along the way!), you can give the rest away and see the results of your kindness produce fruit. I can tell you from experience this is one of the most rewarding aspects of creating wealth. One charity I support is Christian Children's Fund (http://www.ChristianChildrensFund.org). They provide food, medicine, and funding for school for poor kids in Third World countries.

I sponsored a young girl Analiza Dayon in the Philippines for about 7 years through CCF, and in 2003 I was able to visit her with my wife in her hometown. It was a true blessing to know we had helped give her a better chance at succeeding in life and it had only cost us $27 a month.

A famous axiom is "Give a man a fish and you feed him for a day; teach him how to fish and feed him for a lifetime." In light of that wise insight, my favorite charity of all is the Center for Community Transformation (or CCT) www.cct.org.ph. They do microfinance loans, which means they loan money to poor people to start their own businesses in the Philippines. These are people that banks won't lend money to.

Not only does CCT give them a loan when the bank won't, but they're empowering people to own their own business instead of being dependent on a job. And the awesome thing is that they have a 98% repayment rate- 98 out of 100 people they give a small loan to repay the debt! This charity is even more awesome when you consider the high unemployment rate of the Philippines, as it's a Third World country.

I encourage you to develop high standards for the charities you support. My standards are that a charity must 1. be a Christian organization, 2.it must operate efficiently (many charities have 60% or higher overhead), and 3. I prefer charities that empower people to be more self-reliant as opposed to dependent (like CCT that I mentioned). You will likely have different standards than me; be wise with your giving.

As you can tell, I get excited talking about my favorite charities and I'm thrilled to support them generously. When you structure your finances right, you'll be able to not only enjoy your life now but also be able to make a lasting difference in your world.

To recap: Traditional investment advice sucks, plain and simple. It leaves 90% of Americans retiring broke. To avoid this fate and ensure you don't outlive your money, you should first invest in protecting what you already have from lawsuits with proper asset protection.

Then, optimize the return on investment on your money with safe, high-yielding vehicles. You *can* make 20% or more safely. Lastly, leave a legacy for your family and others by creating a Family Bank.

Plan your first Family Bank meeting now!
Life rewards those who take action.

_____ Family Bank Meeting

Dates of meeting: _____

What deposits I will make to the Bank: _____

_____

_____

_____

_____

_____

_____

What we will do on the Fun Day(s) of our
Meeting: _____

_____

_____

_____

_____

**Don't forget to bring a notebook to write
down your experiences (your deposits) for
future generations of the family to learn
from!**

WHY DIDN'T ANYONE *TEACH* ME THIS CRAP?

Chapter 7- How to Create Lifetime Passive Income So You Don't Have To Worry About Losing Your Job

So far we've covered ways to improve the way you think about money, increase your savings and lower your debt, and how to supercharge your investments and protect what you have now.

Now I want to share with you what the rich do to give themselves ultimate security.

Wealth Secret #4: The rich create multiple streams of income that don't require them to keep working to keep earning the money.

I know a woman named Esther who retired a couple years ago. She has been the main supporter of a small local charity for the past 15 years or so, and when she retired the charity's operating budget took a big hit because Esther wasn't earning enough to support it at the level she used to. If she would have remained retired, the charity would have run out of money in 2-3 years.

Well, guess what happened? Can you believe Esther came out of retirement just so she can keep her favorite charity in good shape financially? When I learned of this it blew my mind. Unless the charity gets a more stable foundation of funding sources, they're headed for financial disaster when Esther can no longer work.

What can we learn from this story? It's not wise to rely on just one or even just two sources of income. If one of them goes away, your finances can get into trouble in a hurry.

Sadly, most Americans are in this exact situation. Most families have one or two income streams coming in, and that's it.

How about you? Do you have just one or two income streams coming in? What would happen to you if one of them went away? What if you were laid off, were injured, or one of your businesses folded?

How long would you be able to pay your bills before you were in trouble financially? For most people it'd only be 1-2 months before they were in trouble. This is one of the things I help my clients address as a Wealth Consultant- how to create extra income streams for themselves without a lot of extra work. You can do this too if you want to create ultimate financial protection for yourself and your family.

Before you dismiss this concept, let me tell you one more story. I know a gentleman named Terry who until recently owned a very successful real estate investment company. He has been a successful businessman for over 25 years, and trains others how to build successful real estate businesses as well.

Terry was making over $3 million to $5 million a year in his real estate business and was making money training others how to invest in real estate, and then due to one of his *clients'* mistakes a government agency shut his whole business down. Literally overnight his main income source disappeared!

Terry's training income was a small portion of what he made with his investment company, and when his company was shut down (wrongfully I think, by the way) his income took a rapid reduction. Imagine it- 25 years' worth of building a business gone!

When I talked with Terry after his company was shut down, he was in surprisingly positive spirits. He has mastered the art of utilizing what happens to him in his life, as opposed to just dealing with what happens as most people do. Still he has had to make major adjustments in his life as a result.

What about you? What if 90% of your income disappeared overnight? Or 50% or all of it? Would you like a solution to this?

The good news is that you can take steps to create a stable income foundation for yourself now. If you're willing to grow your thinking about work and money and take action to create multiple streams of income, you won't have to worry about getting into financial hot water as Terry did or as thousands of laid-off automotive workers are in metro Detroit.

So what should you do? For maximum results, do the following (the more of them you do the better your results will be): first decide to create some additional income streams for yourself. Then decide to create those income streams in the **B** quadrant of the Cashflow Quadrant™ mentioned in Chapter 4 (a business that runs without you). Last, automate that business as soon as possible.

To be truly rich, first you have to decide to create multiple streams of income for yourself. Think about Donald Trump- do you think he worries if one of his companies folds? I don't think so. He owns over 23 companies, and he earns income from each one of them. First he decided to create those companies- everything begins in thought. So decide today to create some extra income for yourself.

I council my consulting clients to create three income streams for themselves. The goal is for the income from each stream to cover your monthly expenses. That way if one of them goes away (or is snatched away wrongfully like what happened to Terry), you still have 2 income streams coming in to cover expenses and you can still save money regularly.

The second thing you should do is decide to create those income streams in **true** businesses that will run without you being there (the sooner the better). What kind of business should you start up? There are thousands of choices. I recommend starting a business that combines a profitable business model with what you're passionate about and good at.

Profitable Biz Model + Your Best Skills + Your Passions = A Great Business

Donald Trump and Robert Kiyosaki both recommend network marketing (also known as multi-level marketing) businesses. Most people have had at least one bad experience with network marketing, but before you reject the idea ask yourself a simple question: why does Donald Trump, a billionaire, say if he went broke *today* tomorrow he'd go into network marketing?

There's got to be something to the business model when multibillionaires and business and investing gurus recommend it. Warren Buffet, the most successful investor in history and the second richest man in the world after Bill Gates, owns two different network marketing companies. He's as "old school" as they come, and he sees multi-level marketing as a viable business model.

It's not my job or my aim to convince you to do network marketing. Decide for yourself. I'll give you some pros and cons of the industry to help you make your decision.

There are several good reasons to look into this **B** quadrant type of business.

First of all, if you have no or limited business experience they're a great way to get business training at a bargain price. Most network marketing companies have great training systems that can teach you the skills necessary to be successful in business for only $25 to $100 a month.

I've been in several network marketing companies since my early 20s, and I must say

I've learned many of my best business skills from their training relatively cheaply.

I've bought $10,000 mentoring programs, $5000 real estate seminars, and $3500 business courses; I must admit I've learned just as much from $100 a month training programs in network marketing companies I've been a part of. I've also lost over $20,000 in real estate deals gone bad, so the cost of starting and "failing" in a network marketing business is VERY cheap by comparison. You learn and grow the most from your mistakes, so why not reduce the price tag on your learning curve as you learn what it takes to make it as a business owner?

They're also very cheap to start compared to a franchise. For a few hundred bucks to a few thousand dollars on the high end, you can start a network marketing business that can yield you passive income for years to come. With a franchise, you're often paying $100,000 to $500,000 or more just to get started. That's AFTER you jump through several hoops to qualify to own the franchise and what have you bought? You've bought the "right" to manage teenagers!! Yeehaa!

The low cost to start your own network marketing business is almost laughable it's so low. My friend Steve and I have agreed for awhile now network marketing companies should charge more to get started with them; then people will take their opportunity more seriously like they should.

With ALL that being said, there are some things to watch out for when looking for a network marketing company to join. For one, most of them fail within the first 5 to 10 years. Look for one with at least a 10 to 20

WHY DIDN'T ANYONE *TEACH* ME THIS CRAP?

year track record, one that doesn't require you to make a large upfront purchase of products, and one that has multiple types of products for sale. (some MLMs have only 1 to 5 products for sale- this is a recipe for disaster. See Excel which sold long distance for a historical example. The phone industry changed in the early 2000s, and reps in Excel went from making a killing to making practically nothing really fast)

Dan Kennedy (www.DanKennedy.com) has the best book I've seen on the subject of network marketing called **"Prospecting Sucks."** He mentions 4 key things to avoid in MLMs based on advice from MLM industry attorney Jeffrey Babener. He says to avoid MLM companies that:

1. Offer products with no "real world" marketplace.
2. Offer products with inflated prices

3. Have substantial cash investment requirements

4. Have mandatory purchase requirements

Based on my network marketing experience, I agree with this criteria for any MLM you consider joining. I was a member of a MLM several years ago where you had to invest $5000 to get the best discount. Avoid this.

In the pursuit of full disclosure, I must say that at the time of this writing in 2006 I am currently involved in two different network marketing companies. I'm glad to report they both meet the criteria laid out by the attorney above! I wouldn't have it any other way.

The third step to creating multiple streams of income is to automate your own true business. I've worked at this for over 5 years, and I can say that it's well worth the effort.

For example, in the two network marketing companies I'm involved with one has a 2 to 5 year plan to help its members become "job optional." (earning as much as or more than your job's income from your business passively) I've personally met over 30 people who have retired as a result of this business in the last couple years in the Detroit area alone. These include retired prominent doctors, lawyers, consultants, and professionals.

The other has the ability to help someone become "job optional" in 6 to 12 months, and I have a client who retired from Wal-Mart in under 6 months using this business as part of the financial blueprint I designed for her. This is very rare but it's important for you to know it can be done if you have access to the right business tools and you *use* them.

There are other types of business models and investments that yield consistent monthly cashflow that you can utilize to create multiple streams of income.

If you want the ultimate in financial freedom and protection, I encourage you to decide to join me as a business owner and investor. It will take mental effort and actual work to shift quadrants, and the results will be worth it!

To recap: To create true financial stability for yourself, you must create multiple streams of automated income like the rich do. Three income streams that all exceed your living expenses will put you in a very stable position where if one of the income streams goes away, you still have two income streams to live on.

The easiest way to create these extra income streams is to 1. decide to create them, 2. create the income in the **B** quadrant of the cashflow quadrant, and 3. automate your **B** quadrant business as soon as possible (can be done in 5 years or less). You can invest your excess profits from your business as in investor to create more income streams for yourself!

If you'd like ideas and strategies for creating your own **B** quadrant business, I am available for consulting on a limited basis. Go to **http://FinancialSuccessBlueprint.com/App.html** and submit your application.

If you want to be considered to join either of my MLMs, you must first get the **"Insider Secrets Revealed"** report at http://FinancialSuccessBlueprint.com/CrapBook.html and submit the Questionnaire at the end of the report. **No** whiners or complainers need apply. Only those ready to empower their lives and take action to join the rich should apply.

Chapter 8- Conclusion: So What Does It All Add Up To? That depends on you.

Well, my dear friend, I trust this book has helped open your eyes to the financial mess most people are in. We've been lied to and undereducated about money our whole lives. Our education system has let us down.

Unless we educate ourselves and start taking some different actions, 90% of us are going to retire broke. The way people are living longer and saving less, sadly I think that 90% number is going to go up.

I know I've laid out some radical concepts in this book that defy conventional wisdom; heck, many or most of the ideas I've shared with you may fly in the face of **everything** you've been taught to this point.

I hope I've challenged you to think independently with this book; thinking like the "sheeple" (the vast majority of people who are easily led and simply follow the crowd) will leave you broke and scrambling for financial solutions when it will probably be too late to help you. It's not enough to think; you must now become.

Use the concepts in this book to improve your finances. Start to change the way you think about money and search for mentors to guide you and hold you accountable as you seek a better life for yourself. Spend some time and money to learn about business and how to become an educated investor- an investment in yourself is always worth every penny. Ben Franklin said "Empty your pockets to fill your mind, and your mind will fill your pockets" - likely for the rest of your life!

I trust I've pointed you to enough resources to get the information you need to change your financial path. I want to close by sharing a vital element to your financial success: **ACTION.**

Take action with what you've learned here despite your fear. Fear of failure, fear of success, fear of the unknown- it's all the same and you need to work through it. Every successful person has taken action despite their fears; you're a successful person, aren't you? I thought so.

It's normal to be afraid to try something different. No one wants to be the "odd man out," and I'll tell you now you're going to catch some flack from people around you

when you implement the concepts in this
book. You know what I say? ***Don't take any
of their crap!!***

They're responsible for their results and
you're responsible for yours. Are your family
or friends going to pay your bills for you
when you go broke following traditional
advice? I don't think so; they'll likely be
busy trying to keep their own heads above
water financially. Take responsibility for
your financial future and reap the rewards!

Only 2% to 4% of the people reading this
book will actually take action to improve their
financial situation. Will you be one of them?
Only you can decide.

Welcome to the club, my friend.

You now know the wealth building secrets of millionaires. Now you can proudly say, ***"FINALLY someone taught me this crap!"***

Wala na, kaibigan!!
!Es todo, amigo!

(That's it, friend!!)

THAT'S *ALMOST* IT...

Following is a **Resource Section** containing several of the references I made throughout this book and financial tools for your benefit. Enjoy and put them to use!

WHY DIDN'T ANYONE *TEACH* ME THIS CRAP?

Resource Section

To Optimize The Way You Think:

"Think and Grow Rich" by Dr. Napoleon Hill (Get your FREE copy of this classic at http://FinancialSuccessBlueprint.com/CrapBook.html)

"Rich Dad Poor Dad" by Robert Kiyosaki
"The CASHFLOW Quadrant™" by Robert Kiyosaki
"Rich Dad's Classics" by Robert Kiyosaki
(get all 3 at http://www.RichDad.com)

"Secrets of the Millionaire Mind" by T. Harv Eker
(http://www.MillionaireMindBook.com)

To Track Your Expenses and Savings:

Personal Family Budget Form
(http://FinancialSuccessBlueprint.com/CrapBook.html)

To Live a Balanced Life in Every Way:

"Passion, Profit, and Power" by Marshall Sylver
(www.Sylver.com)

To Protect Your Assets, Reduce Your Taxes (give yourself a 20% instant raise), and Learn How To Invest at 20% or Higher Returns:

"Insider Secrets Revealed" by David Newby
(http://FinancialSuccessBlueprint.com/CrapBook.html)

Resource Section Cont'd.

My Favorite Charities That "Teach a Man How To Fish" (by giving to charity, you set in motion the law of reciprocity; what you give out will always come back to you multiplied):

Center for Community Transformation (www.CCT.org.Ph) - they give small business loans to poor people in the Philippines to help them start their own small businesses. These are people that banks won't give loans to because they "don't qualify" yet CCT has a 98% repayment of loans! CCT also provides loans for affordable housing as well as scholarships for poor students. A charity that is truly empowering people- learn more at their website!

Christian Children's Fund (www.ChristianChildrensFund.org) – they provide necessities of life to poor children all over the world. Be it food, medicine, school supplies, or economic empowerment for the parents of poor children, they provide it. One of the most efficient charities on the planet; in 2005 over 81% of gifts went directly to the children that were sponsored. Awesome! You can sponsor a child for only $24 a month.

Focus on the Family (www.Family.org) – Started by Dr. James Dobson, Focus does radio broadcasts in over 100 countries around the world to strengthen families. A vital charity that brings families closer together when many forces are weakening families.

www.ingramcontent.com/pod-product-compliance
Lightning Source LLC
Chambersburg PA
CBHW022005170526
45157CB00003B/1159